MONKEYS

Snow Monkeys

Mae Woods
ABDO & Daughters

visit us at
www.abdopub.com

Published by Abdo & Daughters, 4940 Viking Drive, Suite 622, Edina, Minnesota 55435.

Printed in the United States.

Cover Photo credits: Peter Arnold, Inc.
Interior Photo credits: Peter Arnold, Inc.

Edited by Lori Kinstad Pupeza

Library of Congress Cataloging-in Publication Data

Woods, Mae
    Snow Monkeys / Mae Woods.
    p. cm. -- (Monkeys)
    Includes index.
    Summary: Describes the snow monkeys of Japan and their food, habitat, and social system.
    ISBN 1-56239-601-3
    1. Japanese macaque--Juvenile literature. [1. Japanese macaque. 2. Monkeys.] I.Title. II. Series: Woods, Mae. Monkeys.
    QL737.P93W67   1998
    599.8'2--dc20

                                   96-11385
                                   CIP
                                   AC

Contents

Snow Monkeys
of Japan

Snow monkey is the common name for the **Japanese macaque**. There are about 50 **species** of macaque. Most of them are **Old World Monkeys** who live in Asia or the islands of the Pacific. The **New World Monkeys** live in the countries of the west. All of these monkeys look alike, but they have different habits and eat different foods.

Japan is made up of four islands. On the largest island, Honshu, there is a range of mountains called the Japanese Alps. This is where snow monkeys live.

This **region** is unlike any other. There are rocky beaches along the shore. Away from the ocean, the soil is rich. The forest is thick with trees and plants most of the year. In the central area, the mountains are steep and rugged.

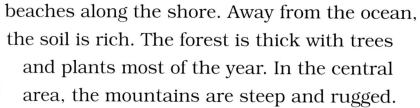

China
Japan

Winters here are harsh. It snows and gets very cold. After the snow **season** sometimes there are **avalanches**. During an avalanche, the mountains shake and waves of rocks and snow slide down the mountainside covering everything on the ground. The monkeys that live in this area are very **resourceful**. Over the years, snow monkeys have learned how to **adapt** to each season.

A snow monkey from the island of Honshu near Japan.

What They Are Like

Snow monkeys have long, shaggy fur to protect them from the cold. Their coats are pale brown or gray. They have short, stubby tails with a tuft at the end. They are larger than other **macaques**. An adult male weighs 40 pounds (18 kg).

Their faces are pink and hairless. They have long, sharp **canine teeth**. Their vision is excellent. It is better than their sense of smell. These monkeys are also very smart. Though they are good tree climbers, snow monkeys live on the ground. They are able to walk on two legs, but they usually only do this when they are carrying food in their arms. At night, they sleep in the trees, crouched low in the forks of the branches.

Opposite page: Snow monkeys are good tree climbers.

Snow Monkey Troop

Like many monkeys, they live in **troops**. There are about 30 animals in the troop. Other **macaques** live in groups of over 100 but in cold **regions** there is not enough food to feed a group of this size.

There is a **dominant** male leader in each troop. The leader takes his position of power by proving his strength and courage. As he grows old, he may have to fight other monkeys to prove he is still strong enough to lead the troop. Snow monkeys live for 35 to 40 years.

There are other **ranks** of power. There is a female leader and many male monkeys who act as scouts when the group travels. All the others are **followers**.

The dominant monkeys eat first and get their own way. Every animal knows its place in the troop, accepts it, and obeys the leaders. Snow monkeys rarely fight.

If the **troop** becomes too large, one strong male will form a second group. This new troop of snow monkeys will search for new feeding grounds. When they find a good spot, they will make that their new home.

A troop of snow monkeys in a thermal pool.

Fall and Winter

In the fall, September is a month of strong winds and heavy rains. The streams flood. Mud covers the forest floor. The monkeys spend their time sitting in the trees or crouching under rocks to keep dry.

Soon everything dries again. In October the leaves turn colors. The air is fresh and clear. This is the **harvest season**. There is food all around them: nuts, berries, wild grapes, and new plant life. The monkeys do not need to travel to find enough to eat. They are very happy. Winter follows, bringing chilly weather. The snow monkeys grow a long, shaggy gray coat of new fur. Now there is very little food. They eat tree bark, seeds, and any vegetation they can find.

The days grow short and foggy. Soon the snows come. The monkeys huddle together in a circle to keep warm. It is now the leader's job to plow through the deep snow every day making a path for the others as they look for food and shelter.

Snow monkeys grow a long coat of fur for the winter.

The Monkey Troop Journeys

Snow monkeys enjoy the natural hot springs found near the volcanoes. They crouch down in the warm water for hours as the snow swirls around them. Their fur puffs out like a hood around their faces.

In March, the snow melts and the weather becomes warmer. The monkeys come down from the mountains. They find acorns on the ground and leaves to eat. They have lived through another year. Spring will soon bring new life to the **troop** and to the forest.

Opposite page: Snow monkeys enjoying a natural hot spring.

Food

Snow monkeys eat fruit, plants, leaves, bark, grains, **vegetables**, nuts, and insects. They particularly like beetles, grasshoppers, and small animals like frogs and crabs.

They drink water by cupping their hand and dipping it into a stream. Sometimes they wash their food in water before they eat it. They think sea water is better for this than fresh water. The ocean gives fruit a nice salty taste.

The **troop** leader decides where they will go every day to search for food. He leads the march into the forest or takes them on a tree climb. Snow monkeys have cheek pouches so they are able to collect nuts and buds in their mouth while they are in the trees. When their cheeks are full, they come down to the ground to eat.

In the winter when the trees are **barren** there is very little food for them. They will have to eat what they can find in order to **survive**. The monkeys nibble on twigs and pick the winter plant buds from the branches. They even strip the bark off the trees and make a meal of it.

A snow monkey eating a piece of fruit.

Babies

A newborn snow monkey is tiny and helpless. It is only about four inches (10 cm) in length. Its skin is pink with very little hair. It has large pink ears. The baby cannot see at first, but it has well-developed hands that allow it to cling to its mother's fur.

At first, the **troop** ignores the infant as though they are afraid of the strange little creature. But the baby grows quickly. Before long, all the monkeys want to hold it.

When the mother travels in search of food, the baby rides along under her holding onto the fur on her stomach. When the infant is a week old, it will begin to crawl. The mother watches over it as it tries to stand and climb.

The little monkey will be able to walk when it is three weeks old. It also learns how to climb onto its mother's back. Then it can sit and ride on top of her.

The baby snow monkey travels with its mother when looking for food.

As Snow Monkeys Grow

The mother likes to **groom** the baby by stroking its hair and picking out any bits of dirt. Monkeys keep clean by grooming each other. They also enjoy it because it is the only time they touch each other. Adult snow monkeys think of a touch as a **challenge** to fight, so they do not get too close to each other. They are only **affectionate** with each other when they are young.

When babies are four months old, they begin to play with other monkeys in the **troop**. They clasp hands. They like to box and wrestle. Another game snow monkeys like is "tree shaking." In this game they **compete** to see who is the strongest. The players take turns climbing a tree and shaking a branch as hard as they can.

In this kind of play, they learn there is an order in their **troop**. Some monkeys have a higher **rank** than others. If a young monkey's mother is "high-ranking," he or she will **dominate** the other monkeys and become a leader.

Young snow monkeys spend most of their time with their own family. Brothers, sisters, and cousins play together. They will be best friends for life.

A group of young snow monkeys grooming each other.

Glossary

adapt - To change to fit new conditions.

affectionate (a-FEK-shun-it) - Loving.

avalanche (AV-eh-lanch) - Landslide of snow, ice, and rocks.

barren (BEHR-en) - Not producing crops or fruit.

canine teeth - The four longer front teeth used for biting and tearing.

challenge (CHAL-ehnj) - To call to take part in a contest; dare.

compete (kum-PEET) - To take part in a contest.

dominant (DAHM-en-nunt) - Most important or most powerful.

dominate - To control or rule.

followers (FA-lo-ers) - Persons who obey a leader.

groom - To clean and care for.

harvest - The time of year when gathered.

hibernate - To spend the winter in a kind of sleep.

Japanese macaque - Snow monkey.

macaque (muh-KAK) - A short-tailed monkey found in southern Asia, the East Indies, and the Pacific Islands.

molt - To shed skin, hair, fur, feathers, or a shell before getting a new covering.

New World Monkeys - Tree-dwelling monkeys that include squirrel monkeys, howler monkeys, and marmosets.

Old World Monkeys - Ground-dwelling monkeys that include macaques, baboons and colobus monkeys.

plentiful - More than enough.

primates (PRIE-maytz) - A group of animals that includes humans, apes, and monkeys.

rank - A position; a standing on a scale of merit.

region (REE-jen) - Area.

resourceful - Skillful at solving problems.

season (SEE-zen) - Different times of the year: spring, summer, fall, and winter.

species (SPEE-sheez) - A group of animals that are alike in certain ways.

survive - To continue to live.

troop - A group.

vegetation (vej-eh-TAH-shen) - Plant life.

Index